Spotlight on Songwriters

KENDRICK LAMAR

Ursula Pang

CREATED BY Humans

Published in 2027 by The Rosen Publishing Group, Inc.
2544 Clinton Street, Buffalo, NY 14224

First Edition

Editor: Greg Roza
Designer: Michael Flynn

Photo Credits: Cover Adam McCullough/Shutterstock.com; (series background) Yuliya Chsherbakova/Shutterstock.com; p. 5 https://commons.wikimedia.org/wiki/File:Kendrick_Lamar,_Bonnaroo_2012-2.jpg; p. 7 (Dr. Dre) Featureflash Photo Agency/ Shutterstock.com; p. 7 (Tupac Shakur) https://commons.wikimedia.org/wiki/File:2Pac_in_1988_color_upscaled.png; p. 9 Suzan Moore/Alamy; p. 11 Gonzales Photo/Alamy; p. 13 Gary Mather/Alamy; p. 15 Tsuni/USA/Alamy; p. 17 ZUMA Press, Inc./ Alamy; p. 19 Gonzales Photo/Alamy; p. 21 UPI/Alamy.

Cataloging-in-Publication Data

Names: Pang, Ursula.
Title: Kendrick Lamar / Ursula Pang.
Description: Buffalo, New York : Created by Humans, an imprint of Rosen Publishing, 2027. | Series: Spotlight on songwriters| Includes glossary and index.
Identifiers: ISBN 9781534553460 (pbk.) | ISBN 9781534553477 (library bound) | ISBN 9781534553484 (ebook)
Subjects: LCSH: Lamar, Kendrick, 1987---Juvenile literature. | Rap musicians--United States--Biography--Juvenile literature.
Classification: LCC ML3930.L136 P36 2027 | DDC 782.421649092--dc23

Manufactured in the United States of America

Some of the images in this book illustrate individuals who are models. The depictions do not imply actual situations or events.

CPSIA Compliance Information: Batch #CSCBH27. For Further Information contact Rosen Publishing at 1-800-237-9932.

CONTENTS

Young Kendrick

Kendrick Lamar Duckworth was born on June 17, 1987. He has two younger brothers and a younger sister. The Duckworths lived in a poor neighborhood in Compton, California. They were homeless for a small time. Kendrick saw a lot of **violence** in his neighborhood as a small child.

Inspired

Kendrick was first **inspired** to become a rapper when he was 8 years old. He watched rappers Dr. Dre and Tupac Shakur making a music video near his home in Compton. Soon after, Kendrick heard his own voice on a recording. This also inspired him to get into rapping and songwriting.

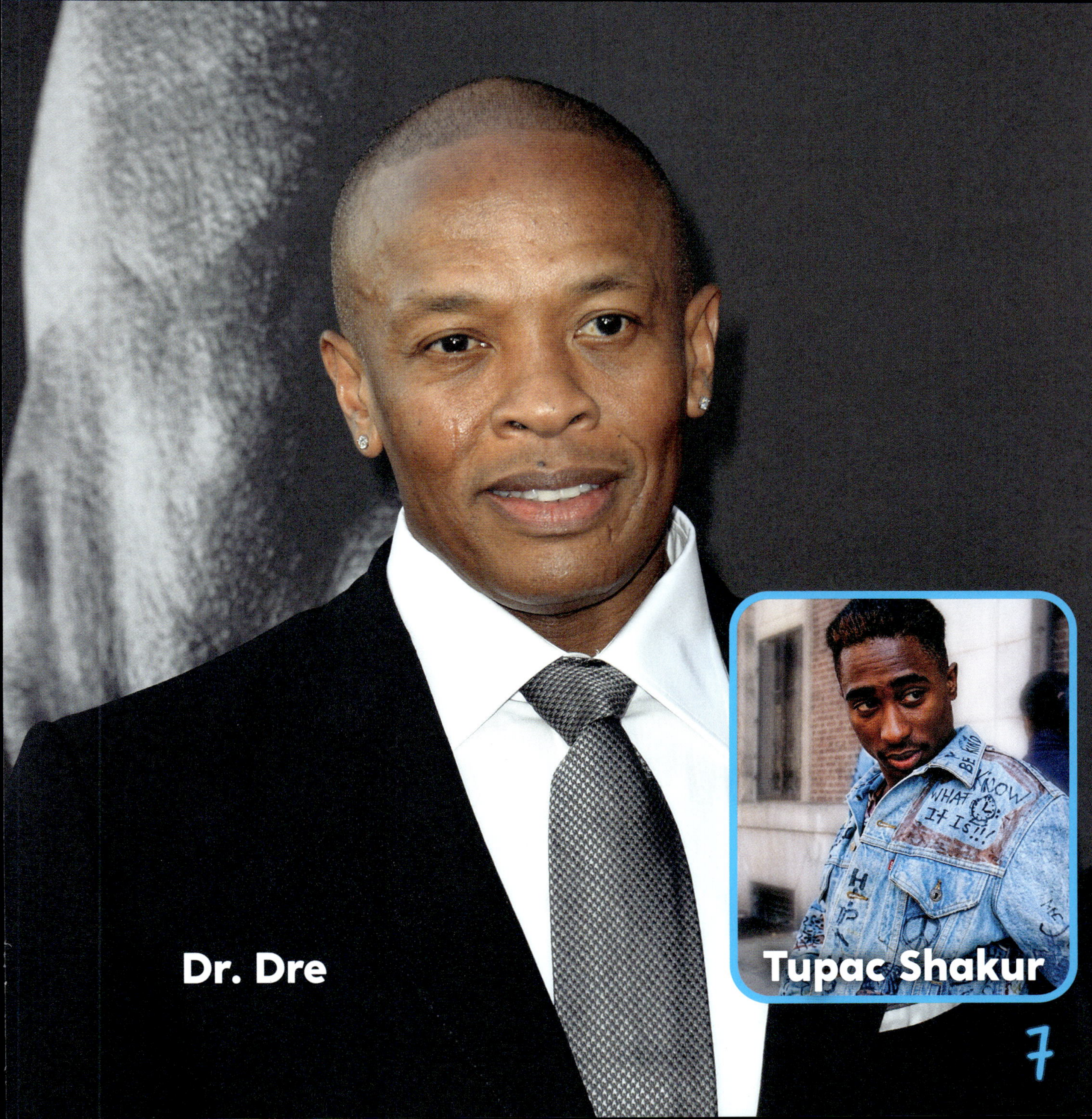

Dr. Dre

Tupac Shakur

Turning to Poetry

Kendrick was a smart boy. He did well in school. However, he was usually quiet because he had a speech problem. Soon he discovered poetry and began to express himself in writing. Kendrick's seventh-grade teacher helped him learn all he could. Soon Kendrick was writing his own poetry.

Mixtapes

In high school, Kendrick began freestyling, or making up rap lyrics on the spot. He joined rap battles in school and often won. Kendrick started performing as a rapper using the rap name K. Dot. He started making **mixtapes** to share with others.

Rising Fame

Kendrick started to make a name for himself in Southern California with his mixtapes. He became one of the first artists to sign with the new record label Top Dawg Entertainment. His first album, *Section.80*, did not sell many copies, but hip-hop artists began to pay attention to Kendrick's work.

Award Winner

Kendrick became more popular with each album he created. His third album in 2015 was a big success. Kendrick used other musical styles on this album, such as jazz. Kendrick won five **Grammy Awards**, including Best Rap Album and Best Rap Song. He even performed at the Grammy Awards that night!

An Amazing Honor

Kendrick released his fourth album in 2017, and it was his biggest success to date. The album won five Grammy Awards. It even won the **Pulitzer Prize** for Music in 2018! Before Kendrick, this award had only ever been given to classical and jazz musicians. It was an amazing honor.

Black Panther

In 2018, Kendrick was picked to produce the music for the movie *Black Panther*. He chose music and artists that he found inspiring. He performed on every song. The song “King’s Dead” won a Grammy for Best Rap Performance. The song “All the Stars” was in the running for an **Academy Award**!

Great Songwriter

Kendrick has worked with many other talented artists. These artists include Taylor Swift, Dr. Dre, Rihanna, and U2. Kendrick performed during the 2025 Super Bowl. It was the most-watched Super Bowl performance ever! Many people think Kendrick is one of the greatest songwriters and rappers of all time.

GLOSSARY

Academy Awards: A yearly award ceremony to honor people who make movies. Also the award itself.

Grammy Awards: A yearly award ceremony to honor people who make music. Also the award itself.

inspire: To give someone an idea of what to create.

mixtape: A collection of songs copied onto a tape, or cassette.

Pulitzer Prize: One of a number of prizes that are awarded in the United States each year for excellent work in writing, reporting, or music composition.

violence: The use of force in a way that harms a person or property.

FOR MORE INFORMATION

BOOKS

Hoffman, Tricia. *Hip-Hop Music*. Buffalo, NY: Gareth Stevens Publishing, 2026.

Knopp, Ezra E. *Hip-Hop and Rap*. Buffalo, NY: Created by Humans, 2025.

WEBSITES

Hip Hop Facts for Kids
kids.kiddle.co/Hip_hop
Learn about the history of hip-hop and find links to numerous hip-hop artists.

Kendrick Lamar Facts for Kids
kids.kiddle.co/Kendrick_Lamar
Read more about Lamar at this detailed website.

INDEX